Original title:
Crocus Cantatas

Copyright © 2025 Creative Arts Management OÜ
All rights reserved.

Author: Vivienne Beaumont
ISBN HARDBACK: 978-1-80566-744-5
ISBN PAPERBACK: 978-1-80566-873-2

Petal-Powered Pas de Deux

Two little bulbus dancers bloom,
With petals bright in springtime's room.
They twirl and spin, a lively show,
In rhythm with the sun's warm glow.

A squirrel joins in, jumps like a king,
With every leap, he starts to sing.
The flowers chuckle, swaying fast,
As sunlight dances, shadows cast.

Bumblebees buzz, join in the fun,
They pollinate, their task well done.
A contest blooms, who is the best?
The daisies laugh, 'We've failed the test!'

The tulip wears a goofy grin,
While daffodils do a silly spin.
All in all, it's quite the sight,
A petaled party, pure delight!

Emergence of Colorful Dreams

A parade of colors, oh what a tease,
They peek from the ground, a playful breeze.
Each flower giggles as it breaks through,
'What took you so long? We've missed you!'

Amidst the blooms, a bunny prances,
In search of treats, he takes his chances.
With every hop, he stirs a laugh,
'Don't mind me, I'm just here for a snack!'

The sun winks down, it's quite the scene,
A canvas painted in shades so keen.
Bees wear hats, butterflies in capes,
As petals sway in silly shapes.

At dusk they yawn, tired from glee,
The flowers whisper, 'What's next for we?'
And under the stars, they dream and scheme,
Of more funny antics in tomorrow's beam!

Colors of Dawn's Embrace

In the garden, colors burst,
Yellow giggles, petals thirst.
Purple whispers, orange prance,
Each flower in a silly dance.

Bumblebees wear tiny hats,
Sipping nectar, doing chats.
Dancing ants with little boots,
Jive along with flowered roots.

Songs from the Garden's Heart

The daisies sing in off-key tunes,
While tulips tiptoe under moons.
Sunflowers sway with arms so wide,
Inviting all for a joyride.

Worms conduct with wriggly flair,
While ladybugs take to the air.
Each bloom chirps a sunny note,
Harmony in every coat.

Harmony of New Beginnings

Springtime hops in like a clown,
With blossoms blooming all around.
Rabbits giggle, chasing tails,
While flowers share their silly tales.

Grasshoppers play acrobats,
Leaping high with sunny hats.
New buds sprout and wave hello,
As laughter makes the garden grow.

Dance of the Sunlit Petals

With every breeze, the petals spin,
A waltz begins, let the fun begin.
In stripes of red and dots of blue,
The garden's laughing, how 'bout you?

Butterflies join in the fray,
Twisting, turning, all the way.
Under the sun, they flip and sway,
In this flower party, come what may.

A Sonnet for the Sun-Kissed

In springtime's glow, they dance with glee,
  With petals bright, as wild as can be.
 They flirt with bees and tease the breeze,
  Each sunny smile, a moment to seize.

 They giggle in colors, a vibrant array,
  Tickling the grass, in a cheerful display.
With laughs that echo as warm winds blow,
 Their charm is a show, putting on a glow.

Kaleidoscope of Petals

A patchwork quilt of shades that rise,
With splashes of joy beneath sunny skies.
They play hide and seek with the wandering bug,
A garden of laughter, a nature-made rug.

Each bloom a prankster, in riotous cheer,
They whisper sweet nothings for all to hear.
With every petal, a story unfolds,
A tapestry bright, in hues bold and gold.

Echoing the Dawn's Chorus

At break of day, the petals yawn,
Stretching their arms, greeting the dawn.
With chirps and giggles in morning light,
They orchestrate joy, a wondrous sight.

They sip on dew, as laughter swings,
In harmony with all the zany things.
A symphony bright, so sweet and spry,
Nature's own band, under the sky.

The Singers of Early Spring

With voices raised, they welcome the sun,
In the key of laughter, oh what fun!
They sway to the rhythm of a warm, soft breeze,
In a festival grand, they shimmy with ease.

Each note a petal that flutters and flies,
Their melodies weave like clouds in the skies.
A choral delight, both silly and sweet,
In early spring's arms, they dance to the beat.

Echoes of the Blooming Heart

In the garden where giggles sway,
Petals blush in a warm ballet.
Bees hum tunes, a buzzing delight,
While ants march in with their tiny might.

A daisy winks, a tulip grins,
Their secret jokes are where it begins.
The morning dew rolls off with flair,
While worms dance, unaware of despair.

The Dance of Morning Blooms

Sunrise reveals a comical sight,
Flowers bob their heads, feeling bright.
A marigold flirts, a sunflower bows,
While daisies discuss their fashionable vows.

The breeze carries laughter through the leaves,
Tickling blooms, tickling thieves.
In this garden of whimsy, all's a jest,
As blooms rehearse for their very best.

Gardens of Gentle Murmurs

Whispers of blossoms, gossip on air,
Petals in chat, who wears what flair?
Lavender's sassy, while roses demure,
A floral debate, both fragrant and pure.

Bumblebees chuckle, bees in a whirl,
Fluttering hopes, a delightful swirl.
Each leaf a witness to soft, tender fun,
Where each little bloom shares a laugh in the sun.

Symphony of the Beacons

In the meadow, a tune begins,
With poppies tapping like old violin spins.
Frogs croak loudly, a comedic beat,
While daisies shimmy to the playful heat.

Fireflies blink in a dance of glee,
As petals sway with humorous esprit.
The night settles in, yet laughter resounds,
In this symphony, joy endlessly abounds.

The Awakening Garden's Anthem

In the dawn's golden cheer,
A flower trips on its rear,
Giggles burst from the soil,
As worms dance with joyful toil.

Bees buzz with a comic flair,
While petals sway without a care,
The sun winks at the grass below,
As shadows play in vibrant show.

Squirrels scatter seeds around,
A jester's leap is the only sound,
Frogs croak in a silly tune,
Hopping to the rhythm of June.

With laughter in every bloom,
The garden's bright with color and gloom,
Underneath the sky so vast,
Nature's joy is unsurpassed.

Veils of Color and Sound

A tulip dons a funny hat,
While daisies form a chatty mat,
Colors clash in wild ballet,
The garden's stage, come what may.

Worms don shades of green and brown,
As ants parade in a tiny gown,
A symphony starts with a thrum,
And daisies beckon, 'Here we come!'

Petals flutter with laughter's grace,
Each blossom joins the silly race,
In the breeze, whispers abound,
As nature's jokes can be profound.

The sun and moon twirl round the sky,
A comedic duo up high,
In this garden of vibrant glee,
Life's punchline is wild and free.

Whispered Notes of the Earth

The soil giggles soft and low,
As seeds with a funny twist do grow,
Whispers dance on the breezy trails,
While frogs sing with flappy tales.

Crickets chuckle in the dusk,
Emitting tunes of earthy musk,
A snail slides by in perfect style,
With a grin that lasts a while.

Laughter bubbles in every nook,
From squishy mud to a shady nook,
Nature hums a merry tune,
Jokes that bounce beneath the moon.

Each leaf joins in, a giggling crew,
Creating songs both bright and new,
A melody through roots and beams,
Life's orchestral, stitched with dreams.

Ballet of Blooming Life

In the garden, a ballet begins,
With petals pirouetting in spins,
Each bloom takes its silly stance,
Nature's whimsy leads the dance.

Bees buzz in rhythm, a cheeky troupe,
As butterflies glide in the loop,
A feat of grace, a fluttering show,
Where the slightest breeze makes them glow.

Underneath the tulip's light,
Insects jiggle, a joyful sight,
Their tiny giggles fill the air,
As blossoms sway without a care.

Oh, the joy when springtime's here,
Each bloom appears with silly cheer,
In this ballet, life finds its way,
A funny show for Earth to play.

Rebirth in the Garden's Embrace

In the soil, a sneeze comes near,
Tiny buds peek, what a cheer!
Color bursts with a chuckling face,
Nature's joke in a cozy space.

Bumblebees dance in the air,
Wiggly worms give a cheeky stare.
They gossip under sunny skies,
While one green shoot dons a tie!

Raindrops tiptoe on petals bright,
Splish-splashing in pure delight.
Each bloom giggles at the sun,
Saying, "Look at me, I'm number one!"

Grasshoppers don their spring attire,
Mimicking cats who jump higher.
With every leap, a laughter grows,
In a garden where silliness flows.

A Tonic of Floral Tunes

Petals strum like a guitar,
A bouquet that's a rock star!
Lilies hum a jovial tune,
While daisies dance beneath the moon.

In the breeze, notes swirl and glide,
Tulips giggle, not one to hide.
The violets join with a wink,
Making everyone stop and think.

Whimsical colors paint the sky,
Sunflowers wave, oh my, oh my!
Gardeners trade their shovels for songs,
As laughter fills the air all day long.

With nature's chorus, laughter swells,
In this place where joy just dwells.
Each flower sings, a silly spree,
Creating a sweet symphony.

The Mixtures of Spring's Alchemy

In a pot of soil, a wizard toils,
Mixing chuckles with garden spoils.
Seeds burst forth in a comical show,
Each petal shakes in a silly glow.

The daisies whisper secrets loud,
Bouncing around beneath the cloud.
While tulips joke about their height,
Poking fun at the mallow's plight.

Silly squirrels with acorn hats,
Prance about like well-fed rats.
In every corner, laughter stirs,
As nature shakes off winter's blurs.

With each bloom stepping out in style,
Spring's alchemy continues to beguile.
In the playground of weeds and greens,
Laughter reigns where joy convenes.

Vibrant Echoes in Quiet Places

Among the shadows, whispers play,
Petals gossip throughout the day.
With every rustle, a jest is made,
In solitude, a laugh parade.

The tranquil pond holds a smirk,
As frogs in tuxedos start to lurk.
They croak their jokes with such finesse,
In their world, it's pure happiness.

The shyest bloom gives a little wave,
While snails race, oh what a rave!
As bumblebees paint with buzzing sound,
In this realm where mirth abounds.

Each corner holds a gentle giggle,
Even the trees dance with a wiggle.
In these vibrant echoes, we find,
That joy persists, intertwined.

Unfurling Dreams in Purple Hues

In gardens where the flowers play,
The purple blooms greet the day.
They dance with joy, they laugh with glee,
A silly sight for all to see.

With petals wide, they wave hello,
While bees buzz by, conducting show.
A sunny stage for petals bright,
As butterflies join in delight.

They poke their heads, a peek-a-boo,
And gossip with the morning dew.
These jolly buds, so spry and free,
Sharing secrets of the bee.

So if you see a patch of cheer,
Just stop and smile, lend an ear.
For flowers sing a joyful tune,
Beneath the laughter of the moon.

Nature's Lullaby in March

March comes in with a giggle,
As seedlings start to wiggle.
The sun peeks out, a cheeky grin,
Inviting all to join the din.

A windy waltz, a breezy tease,
Makes trees do the happy sneeze.
Birds chirp jokes from high above,
While clouds float by, a fluffy love.

Down in the soil, worms tell tales,
Of muddy fun and rainy gales.
They wiggle fast, a slimy dance,
In nature's play, they take a chance.

So if you see a flower bloom,
Don't be shy, dance with the zoom.
Nature's laughter is all around,
In March's joy, let's all be found.

The Fragrance of Hope Reborn

A splash of color here and there,
As scents of spring fill the air.
With blooms emerging, new and bold,
They share their tales of warmth retold.

The daisies giggle in the breeze,
While tulips toss their heads with ease.
Each petal wears a fragrant crown,
Chasing away the winter frown.

Forget-me-nots whisper sweet lies,
As dandelions reach for skies.
With each new sprout, a chuckle found,
In every garden, joy is crowned.

So take a whiff, let laughter swell,
In nature's shop, there's much to tell.
With humor wrapped in every bloom,
Hope blooms, dispelling the gloom.

Velvet Touch of Spring's Arrival

Spring tiptoes in on velvet feet,
With gentle whispers, oh so sweet.
She tickles grass, the flowers beam,
In softest hues, they start to dream.

A lilac laugh, a daffodil shout,
The garden's fun is what it's about.
Bumblebees in a clumsy flight,
Bring laughter to the sunny sight.

The daisies play a game of catch,
While frogs croak 'round the garden patch.
With every sprout, a giggle grows,
As life awakes and joy bestows.

So come along, let's skip and spin,
As spring's warm touch invites us in.
In every bloom and every song,
Spring's velvet touch can't steer us wrong.

A Palette of Joyful Notes

In fields where giggles bloom,
A painter's brush meets flower's plume.
With hues of laughter, bright and spry,
They dance beneath the giggly sky.

Petals jive, a silly chat,
In swirls of colors, where do we sat?
A polka dot parade in sight,
They tickle noses, pure delight.

Bees hum tunes of buzzing glee,
While daisies join in harmony.
A serendipitous delight,
Who knew a garden could feel so right?

In every bud, a chuckle hides,
As morning's warmth and joy abides.
A kaleidoscope of laughs unspun,
A palette where all hearts run.

Rustic Revelries in Bloom

In gardens where the sunflowers wink,
The veggies converse—what do they think?
Radishes giggle, carrots crack smiles,
As the cabbage rolls with its cabbage styles.

Mirth in the melon patch bounces about,
While pumpkins wear hats, are they in doubt?
Each leaf in laughter, a festival cheer,
The tomatoes blush, 'We're ready, my dear!'

The beets tell tales, a vibrant plot,
Of secret dances in the forgotten lot.
With every sprout, a grin to share,
Rustic revelries fill the air.

Then out pops a bunny, with a silly hop,
Dressed in blooms from the garden crop.
Nature's jesters, a playful crew,
In this rustic wondrous view.

Colorful Verses of the Earth

Here in hues that tickle the soul,
Blooms break out with a vibrant roll.
Sun-kissed petals recite their plays,
In colors that sing through sunny days.

Whimsical tulips tease the breeze,
While violets giggle, if you please.
A whimsical world, a flourish spree,
With petals and pollen in jubilee.

From bumblebees buzzing silly songs,
To butterflies dancing all day long,
The earth is a canvas, bright and free,
Painting joy for you and me.

As shadows play where lilies sway,
With laughter echoing through the day.
In this garden of colorful beats,
Life's quirky rhythm humbly repeats.

The Dawn's Floral Choir

The dawn breaks out with a giggly cheer,
As flowers wake, the chatter we hear.
With petals like singers, they lift their heads,
In a floral choir, laughter spreads.

A daffodil announces the day's first joke,
While tulips tell tales that make us poke.
The sun grins wide, its warmth a delight,
As blooms beat time, in morning's light.

Nectar sippers, the bees join in,
With buzzes that hum as they begin to spin.
A comical waltz of colors bright,
In the choir of dawn, a joyful sight.

So let us linger in this bloom-filled song,
Where every petal knows they belong.
With laughter entwined in every note,
The dawn's floral choir keeps hearts afloat.

The First Notes of March

As winter winks and packs away,
The snowman sighs, "I've had my play!"
With boots that squeak on thawing ground,
Spring sneaks in with a silly sound.

The birds return with gossip loud,
They chirp and chirp, so very proud.
While flowers peek from slumber's dream,
They giggle, whispering, "We'll beam!"

The sun plays tag with fluffy clouds,
The world erupts with cheerful crowds.
With every sprout a laugh appears,
March winds bring chuckles, cheers, and cheers.

Bumblebees buzz in a dance so sweet,
While ladybugs march on tiny feet.
Nature's jesters take center stage,
In this playful, vibrant spring-age.

Lullaby for the Awakening Field

The field yawns wide, a sleepy chore,
As sprouts emerge to see what's in store.
With a little sun and plenty of cheer,
They hum soft tunes that all can hear.

Worms wiggle in a wobbly race,
While daisies giggle in their warm place.
The grass bows down to share the joke,
As daisies whisper, "Here comes the oak!"

The clouds float by with cottony sighs,
Painting blue canvas 'neath sunny skies.
Frogs croak lullabies from their bog,
While tiny ants march like a fog.

The joyful soil cracks a wide grin,
As flowers stretch, ready to begin.
With every rustle, the world awakes,
A funny dance that nature makes.

Nature's Vibrant Overture

From croaking ponds to buzzing bees,
The world erupts with raucous tease.
Each bud that bursts is on a quest,
To bring forth laughter—nature's jest!

The trees sway gently, hands in air,
As they dance freely without a care.
Squirrels juggle acorns, what a sight,
As blossoms bloom, a pure delight.

The sunbeam's tickle, laughter flows,
While ants parade in perfect rows.
A rabbit hops, then takes a bow,
As daisies giggle, "Look at us now!"

In vibrant colors, life takes flight,
With jokes and jigs from day to night.
Nature's overture, vibrant, wild,
Brings forth a giggle from every child.

Rhapsody in Bloom

In gardens bright, the flowers sing,
With petals waving, "Look at spring!"
They spin and twirl with sheer delight,
A rhapsody of color in the light.

The tulips chat, the roses laugh,
In this blooming scene, a joyful giraffe.
Dance like a daisy, sway like a fern,
In nature's concert, there's much to learn!

The bumblebees play a buzzing tune,
While butterflies float like a happy balloon.
With every bloom, a story is spun,
As nature winks, "Oh, this is fun!"

In fragrant air, the laughter swells,
With quirky tales the meadow tells.
A rhapsody alive, a vibrant heart,
In this spring show, all play their part.

Musical Notes of Renewal

Spring hops in, so spry and bright,
With flowers dancing, oh what a sight!
The sun's a player on nature's stage,
Each bloom a note, a lively page.

The bees are buzzing, making a chart,
A symphony played by the garden's heart.
Butterflies twirl with a giggle and spin,
Nature's orchestra, let the fun begin!

Melody of the Ground's Awakening

Beneath the soil, a tickle, a tease,
Waking from dreams, the bulbs start to sneeze.
They shout "Surprise!" with colors so bold,
Nature's joke, the best story told.

The trees shake off their winter sleep,
With branches jiving, they sway and leap.
"Come join the party!" they cheer and sway,
As laughter dances, it's a glorious day!

Tapestry of Spring's Whisper

Petals in pajamas, what a sight to see,
Chasing sunbeams, wild and free.
Each flower giggles, a prankster's delight,
Creating a patchwork, oh what a sight!

Grass tickles toes, a playful tease,
The garden hums with buzzing bees.
Nature's canvas, all painted with glee,
A tapestry of joy, just let it be!

The Brightest Notes of the Season

With every sunrise, a jingle in the air,
Buds burst open with flair and care.
Squirrels dance, they spin and twirl,
Spring sings its song, giving life a whirl.

Rains drop like drum beats, splash and play,
Nature's rhythm brightens the day.
"Join us!" they giggle, in this grand ballet,
In harmonies of laughter, we jump and sway!

Petals Paint the Dawn

In springtime's dance, the flowers play,
With petals soft, they greet the day.
They tickle bees, who giggle in flight,
As blossoms blush in morning light.

The gardener trips on his own hose,
While merry buds begin to pose.
They wink and nod, a vibrant chat,
As squirrels laugh, and wear a hat.

Each bloom's a jest, a funny sight,
They tease the sun with sheer delight.
A canvas bright, with greens and golds,
Nature's jokes, in colors bold.

As bumbles hum some silly tunes,
A chorus sung by dancing blooms.
In gardens lush, where laughter flows,
The world awakes to nature's prose.

Harmonies of Awakening

The morning sings with cheerful glee,
While flowers stretch and sip their tea.
They share old tales of bumbles swooning,
In symphonies of bees a-tuning.

Petaled jesters, a sight to see,
Prancing 'round like they're on spree.
They tickle tulips, make them sway,
And wear their smiles the whole long day.

Daffodils laugh, their heads held high,
With sunny hats that touch the sky.
They whisper secrets of playful bees,
In whimsical winds that tease the trees.

As day unfolds with joyous strife,
Each bloom rejoices, celebrating life.
With every swirl, a giggle rings,
Nature alone knows how to sing.

Sunlit Serenades

Beneath the sun, the daisies spin,
In flirty shades, they laugh and grin.
They sway to tunes of morning's call,
In a grand show, they give their all.

Wink to the clouds, a silly game,
While butterflies play their fluff-filled fame.
They twirl and flutter, with joyful flair,
A parade of colors, floating in air.

The daisies sing a chorus bright,
While crickets join in pure delight.
Each petal isn't shy or timid,
In nature's jest, they're all unlimited.

As shadows stretch and laughter flows,
With giggles soft, the garden glows.
Each sunlit song an ode so sweet,
To cheer and charm, a playful feat.

Beneath the Velvet Sky

Under the twinkling stars so bright,
Flowers chuckle in the night.
With moonbeams dancing on their heads,
They share tall tales from cozy beds.

The violets hum a goofy tune,
As fireflies steal the spotlight soon.
With laughter shared, they twirl and glide,
In midnight's glow, they turn the tide.

Petals whisper secrets soft,
Of garden mischief, aloft.
They play hide-and-seek with the breeze,
Tickled pink, they giggle with ease.

The sun will rise, but for now,
They soak in joy, take a bow.
In the velvet night, laughter rings,
Nature's jokes are wondrous things.

A Dance of Colors and Light

In a field where flowers gleam,
Colors swirl, a vibrant dream.
Bees are buzzing, oh what fun,
Dancing petals in the sun.

Bright yellow, purple, and blue,
Each flower's got a wacky view.
Tiptoeing on the grassy stage,
Nature's laughter, all the rage.

Frogs in hats croak silly tunes,
While squirrels dance beneath the moons.
The wind, it giggles as it sighs,
Bringing joy in playful ties.

A parade of blooms in line,
Nature's jesters, oh so fine.
With every sway and every clap,
Funny hats and flower caps.

Serenading the Sunlit Horizon

Underneath the warming skies,
Flowers sing, it's no surprise.
Sunbeams tickle every petal,
Laughter born from nature's mettle.

Beetles march in perfect time,
To the rhythm of nature's rhyme.
Butterflies wear tiny shoes,
As they flit in joyful hues.

A sunflower takes a bow,
While daisies dance, just look at how!
Each twirl sends the shadows flying,
In this dreamy field, all's complying.

With pollen floating through the air,
The world's a stage, so loud and rare.
Nature's band with leaves and sprout,
Creating tunes that laugh and shout.

Flourishing Harmonies

Blossoms burst like giggles bright,
Laughter painting pure delight.
Tulips don a polka dot,
While grassy stage serves as their spot.

Each bloom winks with cheeky grace,
Inviting squirrels to join the race.
The daffodils break out in song,
In the garden where all belong.

With bouquets swaying side by side,
Windy whispers, flower pride.
The crickets keep a steady beat,
As petals tap in joyful heat.

A playful breeze is in command,
Directing sunlight's funny band.
In the garden, where life invites,
Lively verses in nature's flights.

Landscapes of Lively Lyricism

A vibrant patchwork on the ground,
Where laughter of the blooms is found.
Each krokus with a playful jest,
A funny flower in its dress.

With butterflies that almost trip,
On petals soft as jokes they flip.
Bumblebees buzz a comic tune,
While daisies sway and laugh at noon.

The raindrops join the merry band,
Dancing to the beat so grand.
Each splash a giggle in the dew,
That sparkles brightly, fresh and new.

So here's the tale of flowery mirth,
A joyful plot upon the earth.
Where every bud with humor sings,
And nature wears her funniest things.

Petals in the Early Light

In gardens wide, with laughs so bright,
    Petals peek out, oh what a sight!
They dance around, in morning mirth,
    Unfolding joy, a playful birth.

With waxy leaves, they jig and twirl,
    As bees arrive, in joyous whirl.
A flower parade, they wiggle and sway,
    What a goofy start to the day!

One little bloom, with a cheeky grin,
    Says, "Look at me, come join in!"
The sun shines down, awash with cheer,
    Ignoring frost, they persevere.

Petals blushing in early sight,
Laughing at winter, "Take flight, take flight!"
Oh what a comedy, nature's own show,
    In each tiny bud, a giggling glow.

Symphony of the Hidden Bulbs

Beneath the snow, a hidden beat,
A symphony below, what a treat!
The bulbs conspire, with jokes to share,
Telling the moles, "Don't come down here!"

They wiggle and snicker in cozy cliques,
Plotting their growth, with clever tricks.
"Early risers, watch us surprise!,"
They whisper secrets, beneath frost's guise.

When springtime waltzes, they burst on scene,
With bright little gowns, pure and keen.
Their funny hats, all mismatched styles,
A floral revue, bringing forth smiles.

Nature's orchestra, played with glee,
Bulbs holding hands, in harmony.
With each sunny note, they jump and prance,
In a vibrant jig, a floral dance!

Flourish of the Bold Colors

A splash of color, what a display,
Bold and bright in a tricky ballet.
A purple hat and a yellow tie,
These flowers whisper, "Oh my, oh my!"

They paint the fields, like clowns in a show,
Each petal a jester, with quite the glow.
Red cheeks of laughter, green shoes in tow,
Who knew they had such comedic flow?

The colors clash in a playful spree,
A whimsical fight for who'll be the key.
"No, I'm the star," says Mr. Blue,
And Mrs. Pink laughs, "I'm funnier too!"

Spring's joke is simple, a palette bright,
In the garden stage, all take flight.
With petals bright and laughter galore,
What a wild circus, you can't ignore!

Awakening the Winter's Veil

Beneath a quilt of chilly white,
The flowers chuckle, ready to fight.
"Enough of winter," they each declare,
"Let's lift the veil, let's show some flair!"

They poke their heads from frozen ground,
With daring hearts, joy unbound.
"Move over, snow," they shout with glee,
"Make way for fun, come dance with me!"

The squirrels giggle, a curious cheer,
As blooms all gather, spreading good cheer.
They share their tales of the days gone cold,
In colorful whispers, bold and bold.

So here they rise, in sweet rebellion,
Flower power, a bright rebellion.
In laughter's warmth, they break the chill,
Awakening spring, with vibrant will.

The Chime of Colorful Growth

In springtime's dance, a sight so bright,
The flowers giggle in morning light.
A purple bloom wears a sunny grin,
As bees do waltz, they twirl and spin.

The blossoms chat with glee and fun,
While seedlings peek out, all on the run.
A garden party starts to grow,
With petals bouncing to and fro.

In the soil, worms wiggle with flair,
While butterflies prance in fragrant air.
A joke's exchanged between the stems,
As laughter fills the vibrant gems.

So here's to blooms, a merry crew,
With colors bright and skies so blue.
In nature's rhyme, we sing along,
A joyful tune, a garden song.

Hymns of the Garden's Awakening

Under the sun, they start to shout,
The daffodils wearing yellow hats about.
They tease the tulips, oh what a sight,
A floral choir in pure delight.

The daisies laugh, a playful bunch,
As squirrels join in for a lively lunch.
With every petal, a silly jest,
Nature's humor at its best.

The robin sings a cheeky tune,
As frogs hop frogs, 'neath the bright full moon.
Each leaf a dancer, bold and quick,
As shadows prance with a funny flick.

A garden's hymn, a merry sound,
Where joy and laughter can be found.
In nature's jest, the heart takes flight,
With every bud ushering in delight.

Emotive Cadence of the Green

The green parade starts in a rush,
With leaves that giggle, and branches that blush.
Each stem a player in nature's game,
Yet all of them insist they're not the same.

Silly petals toss and tease,
With bees that buzz, like they're on a spree.
A tulip trips, falls on its face,
While roses roll, mischief in place.

With morning dew, they slip and slide,
As ladybugs laugh, full of pride.
Each sprout a jester, bold and bright,
In this colorful chaos, pure delight.

In the woodland, a ruckus ensues,
With nature's jokes, one cannot lose.
So dance along, take part in the fun,
For every bloom shines just like the sun.

The Nutriments of Nature's Aria

The soil hums a tune so fine,
With roots that wiggle in wild design.
They sip the sunshine, a silky drink,
With every drop, they giggle and wink.

The fertilizer sings in joyous tone,
While earthworms wiggle, never alone.
A chorus rises from up above,
As clouds play tricks, like a child in love.

In the garden's heart, a banquet laid,
With veggies chattering, none are dismayed.
Each sprout and bloom, a banquet guest,
Raising their leaves as they jest and jest.

So come and join this merry spree,
Where every shade tells tales of glee.
In nature's aria, we find our place,
In laughter's rhythm, a warm embrace.

Flourishing under the Sun

In a garden full of cheer,
Tiny blooms start to appear.
They dance and twirl, oh what a sight,
Reaching up to catch the light.

Bees buzzing like they own the place,
Stealing nectar, what a race!
Petals shiver, ticklish glee,
Nature's giggle, wild and free.

Worms in suits, with top hats worn,
Wiggle to the break of dawn.
Grassy stage, both green and grand,
Where flowers join the lively band.

Silly plants with pranks to pull,
Winking in the sunlight's lull.
A garden joke, oh what a pun,
Life is wild, and all for fun!

Chorus of the Flowery Dawn

Morning brings a vibrant hum,
Buds pop open, here they come!
Colors clash in playful fight,
Each one's brighter than the light.

Butterflies flutter in fancy dress,
Critters prance without a stress.
A daisy bumps into a rose,
"Oops, excuse me!" laughter flows.

Petunias sing in off-key notes,
While daisies swap the silliest quotes.
A tulip twisted into a grin,
Says, "Life's best lived in a spin!"

Sun beckons, a naughty tease,
For blooms to sway, dance, and please.
Together they sing a merry tune,
A morning show for the sun to swoon!

Heartbeats of a Blossoming World

Little buds with hearts so bold,
Whispering secrets of spring's gold.
Tickled by the softest breeze,
They giggle in their leafy tease.

A tulip totters, a bit too proud,
"Look at me, I'm blooming loud!"
But daisies, in their simpler style,
Chuckling with a cheeky smile.

The violets are in a wild debate,
"Who's the cutest? Come on, mate!"
A rose rolls eyes, just grins and sighs,
"Guys, you're all stunning in disguise!"

As petals drift in playful swirls,
Nature's joy, it dances and twirls.
Each heartbeat feels the warmth and play,
In the garden's sweet, funny ballet!

Strings of Budding Beauty

In the garden, strings are pulled,
As blooms emerge, life is lulled.
A puppet show of nature's art,
Where laughter grows right from the heart.

A daffodil plays the banjo sweet,
While lilacs tap their tiny feet.
A sunflower shouts, "Join the play!"
As petals sway in bright array.

The pansies joke, "What's in a name?"
"You're all the same!" They stake their claim.
But orchids dance with graceful flair,
While all the blooms just stop and stare.

Nature's concert, loud and bright,
With every flower taking flight.
The garden hums, a giggly tune,
Where joy springs forth like afternoon!

Pinks, Purples, and Sunny Sights

Pinks burst forth, a cheeky sight,
Purples dance in morning light.
Buzzing bees with playful flair,
Chasing petals through the air.

Sunshine wraps around each bloom,
Casting shadows, brightening gloom.
Butterflies in dizzy twirl,
Flutter past with joyous swirl.

Garden gnomes in silly hats,
Join the blooms in friendly chats.
Giggles echo, laughter flows,
Nature's joy in vibrant shows.

With every step, a funny phase,
Spring's parade, a lively craze.
Colorful patches, bloom and cheer,
Pinks and purples bring us near.

Melodies from the Heart of Spring

Whistle tones from tiny springs,
Nature's choir, oh, how it sings!
Buds are blooming with a wink,
Life's a stage, don't you think?

Bouncy rabbits, swift and spry,
Hopping 'neath the blue, wide sky.
Squirrels prance with acorn dreams,
In this dance, all's as it seems.

Joyful notes on breezes fly,
Laughter mingles, soaring high.
Melodies that tickle the ear,
Playing tunes we all hold dear.

With each step upon the grass,
Silly things just come to pass.
Hearts are light, us just a fling,
Life's a laugh—a joyful spring!

Whispers of Spring Blooms

Whispers of blooms, soft and sweet,
Underfoot, a lively beat.
Surprises pop in colors bright,
Making every moment light.

Chirping birds with quirky calls,
Dance around the garden walls.
Poking fun at sleepy bees,
Buzzing 'round, oh what a tease!

Daffodils wear grins so wide,
Tickled by the playful tide.
Petal feasts on cakes and pies,
In this world of cheerful highs.

Giggles linger, shadows play,
Springtime bloomers steal the day.
With a wink and silly tune,
Life's a laugh from morn till noon.

Melodies in the Meadow

In the meadow, where laughs collide,
   Giggles hide, nowhere to bide.
Wildflowers sway with playful grins,
   Tickling toes as one begins.

Bees wear shades, so cool and bright,
   While butterflies take flight at night.
Frolicking ants in an endless race,
   Every creature finds its place.

Whisked away on gentle breeze,
   Silly thoughts bring sweet unease.
Nature's joke, a grand ballet,
   Springtime's jest is here to stay.

In this charm, where fun is king,
   Joyful breaths in every swing.
Listen closely, hear the sound,
Of laughter in the blooms around.

The Petal Poets of Spring

In sunny fields, the flowers chat,
With gossip spread on leaves and that.
They crack jokes beneath the sky,
A blooming laugh, oh my, oh my!

The bees, they buzz, a comedic sting,
As daisies dance, they twist and swing.
A tangle of petals, a vibrant crew,
With witty puns that only they knew.

The tulips toss their colorful hats,
While wind whispers, "Hey, check out that!"
With every gust, a ticklish tease,
In the garden, they all aim to please.

So raise a glass to blooms so bright,
With laughter echoing in delight.
For every petal has a tale,
In Spring's embrace, the laughter sails.

An Ode to Nature's Palette

Oh, paintbrush skies and greens so bold,
Nature's strokes never get old.
Each flower struts in vibrant hues,
With color clashes like wild interviews!

The red buds blush, the yellow beams,
Each petal whispers its wild dreams.
The purple laughs, a regal queen,
In this garden, a color scene.

When colors clash, they pout and play,
A marigold sighs, "Why's the rose so gray?"
With petals flapping like silly tunes,
They serenade the waking moons.

So here's to hues that tickle the eye,
In Nature's palette, all colors fly.
A comedy of pigments, they prance and sway,
Creating laughter on a sunny day.

Ballad of Budding Brilliance

In the garden, sprouts arise,
With knobby knees and goofy sighs.
They stretch their stems, a glorious sight,
Budding brilliance, a true delight!

The daisies joke, "We're flowers, not weeds!"
As they dance around in whimsical deeds.
The poppies pop with an energetic cheer,
With petals flapping, they draw near.

The violets giggle in lavender gowns,
While sunflowers boast with towering crowns.
A frolic of colors, united they stand,
In laughter's embrace, they fill the land.

So raise your glass to buds that shine,
With jokes and jests, they intertwine.
In every bloom, a story so grand,
A silly saga of nature's band!

Sonata of the Seasonal Shift

As seasons turn, the flowers play,
The sunflowers cheer—the winter's gray!
With petals swirling, a merry dance,
In spring's sweet song, they take a chance.

The daffodils trumpet with a honk,
While pansies share a cheeky bonk.
From chill to warmth, they blend with ease,
Creating chaos among the trees.

The breeze strums strings of flowing notes,
As blossoms sway in flower coats.
They giggle softly, a floral jam,
In the sunny spotlight, who's the slam?

So let's applaud this vibrant show,
As blooms and buds bring forth the glow.
In this sonata, where humor lifts,
The garden's tune, a nature's gift!

Blossoms in the Winds of Change

Beneath the snow, the secrets lie,
A flower's grin as the frost waves bye.
With petals bright, they dance in glee,
Who knew they'd party so sprightly, whee!

The squirrels prance, they twirl around,
Wearing hats made of leaves they found.
The tulips gossip, the daisies snicker,
As bees buzz by, their jokes grow quicker.

In spring's embrace, the world's a stage,
Old winter's ghost turns the next page.
Nature's whimsy, a vibrant play,
With flowers charades in bright array.

So let the blooms paint every street,
With laughter fresh as springtime's greet.
In every breeze, a joke unfolds,
As flowers giggle, and life retolds.

Vibrations of a Thawing World

As ice melts down, the puddles sing,
The frogs croak jokes, and nature's bling.
The sun's warm smile, a playful tease,
Gives winter chills a soft unease.

The robins boast of their latest finds,
While busy ants form mischievous lines.
A tap dance here, a leapfrog there,
Nature's anthem fills the air.

The tulips tumble in vibrant hues,
Each one telling tales of its own views.
With each new bud, a giggle grows,
In this grand show, the humor flows.

The thawing world spins in delight,
Nature's canvas, a comical sight.
So grab your hats, come play outside,
In this fest of blooms, let laughter glide.

Nature's Flourishing Harmony

In green attire, the trees all prance,
Each branch a dancer, lost in trance.
The flowers chuckle, the earth's a stage,
With every bloom, we turn a page.

Bees with hats plan a buzzing spree,
The daisies wink, as they sway with glee.
A playful breeze tickles the leaves,
In this green world, nothing deceives.

The sun's a jester with rays so bright,
Warming the hearts in morning light.
Each petal whispering comical tunes,
As laughter echoes 'neath the tunes.

Come join the dance, be part of the fun,
With nature's humor, the best under the sun.
In every bloom, a smile awaits,
A harmony crafted by nature's states.

Songs of the Rejuvenated Earth

Hark, the earth sings in merry tones,
With flowers playing on little stones.
The daisies giggle, the roses sway,
In this vibrant choir, they all play.

The brook babbles jokes, the breeze just sighs,
As daisies roll their little eyes.
The grand old oak tells stories of spring,
In each rustle, laughter takes wing.

From seed to bloom, a silly ballet,
As colors burst in a glorious way.
The frogs croak rhymes, insects beeps,
Nature's concert, the laughter keeps.

In morning dew, jokes form and glint,
Nature's humor, a perfect hint.
So come and listen, let your heart twirl,
In songs of spring, the world does whirl.

The Sound of Blooming Life

In springtime's dance, the flowers tease,
A chorus hums, a gentle breeze.
They giggle soft with colors bright,
As bees attempt their clumsy flight.

The garden wakes, a comic show,
With petals launching to and fro.
A tulip tripped, oh what a flair,
While daisies laugh without a care.

Nature's jokes in hues deployed,
In sunlight's warmth, we're all overjoyed.
The blooms unite, a vibrant crew,
With pollen jokes, a comedy new!

So come, dear friend, and take a seat,
Amidst the blooms, a floral feat.
For laughter swells with every hue,
In this bright patch where joys renew.

Ode to Fluency of Flora

In gardens wide, the flowers speak,
With secrets shared, their language unique.
A sunflower yawns, a lily grins,
While petunias gossip about the winds.

Their leafy tales are hard to miss,
As violets wink, it's pure flower bliss.
A rose gave shade, a humor spry,
In every bloom, a hearty sigh.

Dandelions chuckle at every breeze,
Spreading wishes as light as peas.
With blossoms bold, they zoom and twirl,
Creating a ruckus, a floral whirl.

Eavesdrop close, the voices cheer,
For nature's fun is always near.
In petal songs, we find our glee,
A vibrant tune, a flowery spree.

The Glistening Brush of Dawn

At dawn's embrace, the petals glow,
With sparkle fresh, they steal the show.
A daffodil claps, a merry sight,
As morning beams break through the night.

The dew drops bounce like tiny balls,
As morning yawns and gently calls.
A misty breeze, the blossoms dance,
In nature's ball, they take their chance.

Snapdragons grin in pastel hues,
Telling tales, they simply refuse.
With laughter sweet, they twirl around,
In every petal, joy is found.

So waltz in rhythm, join the show,
With blooms that giggle, high and low.
For in this dawn, life's song is clear,
A blooming world brings endless cheer!

Fiction of Flora's Flourish

In tales untold, the blooms declare,
Adventures wild flow in the air.
A tale of vines that learned to fly,
And lilies that giggled as they tried.

A petal ring went on a quest,
To find the sun, they gave their best.
Pansies plotted with rosy schemes,
In flower fables, fun reigns supreme!

With every whisper of the leaves,
Laughter springs, and joy conceives.
A pumpkin's tale, a funny fright,
With oranges laughing in delight.

So turn the page and plant a grin,
These stories twine, where laughs begin.
For in the world of flora's play,
Each blossom's bloom shows life's array.

Serenade of the First Blossom

In winter's grip, they twirl and sway,
These little blooms come out to play.
They peek from snow, a brave debut,
In purple coats, they dance anew.

They tickle ducks with petals bright,
And giggle at the frosty night.
With whispers soft, they tease the sun,
"Oh look, it's spring! Let's have some fun!"

A band of buds, they strut in cheer,
Declaring boldly, "Spring is here!"
Their scented notes float through the air,
As bees arrive with much to share.

So let us sing, make quite a fuss,
For tiny blooms, we all can trust.
With every petal, laughter grows,
In springtime's smile, hilarity flows.

Tunes of the Tender Buds

Little buds with dreams so grand,
They hum along, a flower band.
In rosy hues, they sing their tune,
And shake their heads to greet the moon.

With leaves like hats, they tip in style,
They waltz and dance, they prance awhile.
Oh, listen close, can you hear their cheer?
The blossoms say, "Spring's finally here!"

Their tunes fill the garden, oh so sweet,
With laughter in every rhythmic beat.
"Let's show the world our vibrant flair!"
As petals shake, without a care.

So come and join this merry show,
Where tender buds put on a glow.
With twirling skirts, and laughter bright,
They greet the day, a pure delight.

Vibrance in the Frost

In frosty air, they dare to shine,
With colors bold, they draw the line.
Muffin hats on blooms so spry,
They look at winter with a sly eye.

"Oh chilly breeze, you think you're tough?
But watch us now, we'll strut our stuff!"
In coats of violet, yellow, and white,
They giggle at the morning light.

Their laughter mingles with the frost,
As shimmering gems, they count the cost.
"Will we survive?" the sleepy grass sighs,
But vibrant blooms just roll their eyes.

So raise a toast to blooms that laugh,
In winter's realm, they seize the path.
With every color, joy does frost,
In playful profusions, never lost.

Chorus of Blooming Color

Around the garden, colors clash,
Where hues collide in joyful thrash.
The tiny buds with silken grace,
Create a melody, a floral race.

They hum a tune both bright and loud,
Each petal raising up its proud.
"Dance with us, oh humble bee,
Join in our bright cacophony!"

With every breeze, they sway and spin,
"Let's have a laugh, and let's begin!"
Daffodils whisper jokes to peas,
While tulips tease the busy trees.

A sunny symphony unfolds,
With every color, stories told.
So bloom and laugh, oh heart delight,
In nature's dance, everything feels right.

Singing Blades of Grass

In the meadow, green blades sway,
Whispering jokes in the light of day.
They tickle the toes of passing bees,
Who laugh and dance in the soft spring breeze.

A grasshopper hops, a comedian bold,
Telling tales of the weather, hot or cold.
The daisies giggle, their petals aglow,
Planting puns where the wildflowers grow.

With every gust, the laughter grows,
As snickers float high where the sweet wind blows.
A ticklish sight, oh what a scene,
Nature's own stand-up, reveling in green!

And as the sun sets, a curtain call,
The grass takes a bow, proud and small.
Tomorrow they'll sing, once more in jest,
In this playful world, where all are blessed.

The Awakening Whisperer

A tiny seed stretches, yawns in the light,
Wakes from its slumber, oh what a sight!
With a giggle, it grows, and wiggles about,
Practicing lines from the springtime shout.

The trees roll their eyes, playing hard to get,
As the new sprouts nudge them, no sign of regret.
"Wake up!" they tease, "It's time to shine!"
But the trees just snicker, "We're too divine!"

A dandelion dreams of a fluffy parade,
While tulips sashay, unafraid and unmade.
"Let's twirl in the sun!" they call from the ground,
Spreading laughter like rain, joy unbound.

So come join the prance, in bloom's sweet embrace,
Where whispers of blooming create quite a space.
Let the morning unfold with each giggle and shout,
In a world full of cheer, there's never a doubt.

Pastels in the Morning Light

Ah, the hues of dawn, like a playful tease,
Pastels awaken with a lighthearted breeze.
Pinks and yellows in a color-filled spree,
Even the tulips roll over with glee.

A bluebird hops in, sings a silly song,
While daffodils sway, nodding along.
"Let's paint the town!" whispers shy lilac,
"Using every tone from the garden's backpack."

The sun spills out laughter that colors the air,
Each shade a chuckle, a whimsical flair.
And as the flowers giggle, dance in delight,
They twirl in the sparkles of the morning light.

With each radiant shift and playful hue,
The garden becomes a canvas anew.
In vibrant confusion, joy leaps and spins,
In the art of the dawn, where the laughter begins.

Prelude to a Blossoming World

Beneath the frost, the giggles lie,
Dreaming of blooms beneath the sky.
"Wake up, you slumbering buds," they cry,
"Spring's on the way, come give it a try!"

Little shoots poke through, with a wink and a smile,
Sharing secrets of soil, giggling all the while.
"Here comes the sun, don't stay hidden in fright,
Dance with your colors, and shine oh so bright!"

The earth is a stage, every sprout takes its place,
With petals in makeup and a joyous grace.
"Let's plan for a party!" yells the green grass,
While daisies agree, "We'll make it a blast!"

So let's paint the world with laughter and cheer,
As blooms burst forth, bringing spring ever near.
In this prelude of joy, with rhythm and swirl,
Come join the fun in this blossoming world!

Murmurs from the Earth

In chilly wraps, the bulbs do bide,
Waiting for spring's return to glide.
They giggle and wiggle in the mud,
Whispering secrets, even in the flood.

Tiny shoots peek out with glee,
"Hey, look at us, so bold and free!"
They poke their heads through winter's snore,
Cracking jokes about the frosty floor.

With specks of purple, yellow, and white,
The garden bursts, a colorful sight.
It's a dance of petals, a merry parade,
Each flower's caper, a grand charade.

So here's to the blooms, with laughter grand,
They tickle our hearts, and so we stand.
In this humble patch, joy is found,
With every chuckle, life spins around.

Dawn's Floral Ballad

As dawn breaks out with sleepy yawn,
The flowers wake, and oh, they fawn.
"What's that? Is the sun really here?"
They stretch in jest, all full of cheer.

With petals confused, they sway and spin,
"Should we be shy or wear a grin?"
One says, "Let's throw a morning rave!"
While another scoffs, "Just behave!"

A bee buzzes by, ready to dance,
They giggle and wiggle, given the chance.
Each bloom knows it's a whimsical morn,
In the floral world, no need to scorn.

So here's to petals, bright and loud,
Making mischief, drawing a crowd.
In the light of dawn, they sing and play,
A cheerful anthem to greet the day!

The Color of Renewal

A splash of colors blooming bold,
Each little petal a tale untold.
With sassy grins, they strike a pose,
"Hey, look at us! We're nature's shows!"

From rust to blush, a wild display,
Who knew flowers could be this cray?
With every hue they charm and tease,
Giggling softly in the breeze.

They twirl in gardens, cheeky and bright,
As if to say, "Isn't life a delight?"
Through rain or shine, they bask and bounce,
Laughing at woes, doing their flounce.

In a riot of colors, they find their voice,
Inviting all creatures to join in rejoice.
So let's celebrate, no need for the drear,
With flowers around, there's always cheer!

Awakening the Silent Soil

The earth awakes with a rumbling cheer,
As flowers yell, "Spring's finally here!"
They push through dirt, with a wink and a grin,
"We were just napping, let's get this in!"

With each little sprout that pokes up high,
It seems the ground lets out a sigh.
"Good to see you!" it whispers bright,
"Let's color this world and make it right!"

Tiny roots jive, a silent ballet,
In the soil's embrace, they laugh and play.
"Let's sprout and pout, and shake it all down,
Being colorful jesters, in our leafy crown!"

So here's to the blooms, that brightened the day,
Turning the dull into a vibrant display.
In every petal, a giggle, a tease,
Awakening joy, like a gentle breeze.

An Ode to the Season's Promise

In spring's embrace, the blooms do tease,
Tiny petals dance with ease.
A shy sun peeks through fluffy clouds,
While breezes giggle, drawing crowds.

The bees are buzzing, hats atop,
Chasing blooms, they never stop.
With colors bright and scents so sweet,
They twirl around on tiny feet.

But watch your step, oh silly friend,
For clumsy feet can cause a bend.
A stumble here, a tumble there,
Laughter echoes through the air.

Perennial jesters, in bloom so bold,
Whispering secrets, tales retold.
A merry dance, their spirits high,
In the garden, the jokes comply.

Revelry in Shades of Gold

A riotous splash, not meant to last,
Petals like sunshine, sloshed and vast.
In every corner, they prance and play,
Chasing the chill of the winter's gray.

Potatoes sulk, envy their flair,
While daisies cheer from a cozy chair.
With winks and giggles, they share the stage,
As nature's jesters flip the page.

Toadstools caper, frogs join in too,
A chorus line where nobody's blue.
The merry marigolds lead the dance,
In spiral moves, they twist and prance.

All the critters, feeling grand,
Join the revelry, hand in hand.
To the raucous tunes of springtime's boast,
They toast, they cheer, a joyful host.

Tuning into Earth's Refreshing Notes

With each new bloom, the chorus wakes,
Nature's band, oh what a mix!
From rustling leaves to chirps so bright,
They serenade the fading night.

A rabbit hops, does a jig, so spry,
While worms compose a squirmy sigh.
The wind's a conductor, waving its wand,
Creating symphonies, wild and fond.

Let's don our hats and join the show,
With silly moves, we steal the flow.
They tap their feet, we twirl around,
Creating laughter — a joyful sound.

As daisies chime and tulips sing,
The earth rejoices in everything.
A waltz of colors, harmony reigns,
In nature's concert, joy remains.

Gentle Murmurs of Duration

Time slips in with a gentle sway,
Tickling petals along its way.
These fleeting moments wrapped in cheer,
Whisper of laughter, echoing near.

Oh, the squirrels, with antics galore,
A clumsy leap, then rolling on the floor.
With every giggle and every fall,
They remind us, we should have a ball.

Sunshine chuckles, casting a grin,
While puddles giggle, inviting a spin.
The fleeting spring, with a playful tease,
Keeps us guessing, as it aims to please.

So let us dance through these sunny days,
In whimsical steps, in joyful ways.
For each gentle murmur, a tale to unfold,
Of laughter, of life, eternally bold.

First Light over Tainted Ice

In the dawn, a jester skates,
Tripping on the sunlit plates.
Laughter echoes, ice does crack,
Wonder if he'll make it back.

Frogs in toques play leapfrog games,
As snowflakes whisper silly names.
A snowman's head rolls down the hill,
Chasing giggles, what a thrill!

Sunshine winks, a playful tease,
Melted winter, joys to seize.
Orange socks on penguins strut,
Chaotic fun, oh what a rut!

With each slip and spicy joke,
The icy world begins to smoke.
First light brings a chuckle's dance,
Tainted ice, a merry chance.

A Palette of Tender Revival

Colors burst from sleepy earth,
Grumpy gnomes proclaim their worth.
Painting daisies, pinks, and blues,
While the sun spills mugs of hues.

A rooster sings a silly tune,
While tulips sway and sneak a swoon.
Bees wear shades, oh such a sight,
Buzzing, dancing, pure delight.

Pansies giggle, petals shake,
The daffodils all start to bake.
A rainbow runs with squeaky shoes,
Chasing after moonlit crews.

In this garden, laughter blooms,
The colors chase away the glooms.
A palette mixed with flair and fun,
Tender revivals for everyone!

The Awakening of Sleeping Gardens

Sleepy buds, a yawning spree,
Stretching wide and sipping tea.
Worms in pajamas wiggle tight,
Preparing for the morning light.

Toads in slippers hop around,
While daisies do a dance profound.
Butterflies wear party hats,
As flowers chat like chubby cats.

A snoozing bee snores in the rose,
Dreaming of pollen, sweet repose.
Tulips laugh with silly faces,
In gardens spun with funny races.

Awakening, this lively scene,
Nature joins the comedy routine.
Gardens wake from slumber deep,
Tickled greens, no time for sleep!

Chorus of Colors at Daybreak

Morning waltzes in with cheer,
A rainbow sings, oh what a year!
Clouds in stripes like candy canes,
Whispering laughter through the lanes.

Chirping crickets, lead the tune,
While daisies twirl under the moon.
Sunflowers giggle, swaying wide,
As colors rush, they cannot hide.

The sky, a canvas, fills with dreams,
Every brushstroke bursting at the seams.
Bumblebees with rhythm sway,
Buzzing loud, come join the play.

In this chorus, hearts all blend,
Colors dance, the fun won't end.
A daybreak song, so bright, so bold,
In laughter's warmth, pure joy unfolds.

www.ingramcontent.com/pod-product-compliance
Lightning Source LLC
Chambersburg PA
CBHW051635160426
43209CB00004B/665